Catholic Enrichment Activities for
Mother Mary Loyola's

The King of the Golden City
An Allegory for Children

A RACE for Heaven Study Guide

by Janet P. McKenzie. OCDS

Biblio Resource Publications, Inc.
Bessemer, MI

© 2001, 2009 by Janet P. McKenzie
Second Printing 2015

ISBN 978-1-934185-04-9

Cover photo © free_photo – Fotolia.com

Published by
Biblio Resource Publications, Inc.
108 ½ South Moore Street
Bessemer, MI 49911
www.BiblioResource.com

Printed in the United States of America

The King of the Golden City, An Allegory for Children Study Guide

Table of Contents

Spiritual Read-Aloud

Spiritual Reading

In *My Daily Bread, A Summary of the Spiritual Life* by Father Anthony Paone, S.J., Christ tells us,

> My Child, reading and reflecting are a great help to your spiritual life. My doctrine is explained in many books. . . . Some of these books are written simply, and some are very profound and learned. Choose those which will help you most toward a greater understanding and appreciation of My Truth. Do not read to impress others but rather to be impressed yourself. Read so that you may learn My way of thinking and of doing things.

In her book, *Saint Dominic, Preacher of the Rosary and Founder of the Dominican Order*, Mary Fabyan Windeatt quotes St. Dominic as saying, "A little good reading, much prayer and meditation . . . and God will do the rest." Fr. Peter-Thomas Rohrbach, OCD, states that spiritual reading is the "third essential asset for mediation" (after detachment and recollection). The great value he places on the habit of spiritual reading is expressed in his book *Conversation with Christ, An Introduction to Mental Prayer*:

> We live in a world devoid, in great part, of a Christian spirit, in an atmosphere and culture estranged from God. Living in such a non-theological environment makes it difficult for us to remain in contact with the person of Christ and the true purpose of life itself. We must, if we are to remain realistically attached to Christ, combat this atmosphere and surround ourselves with a new one. Constant spiritual reading fills our minds with Christ and His doctrine—it creates this new climate for us.
>
> In former ages, spiritual reading was not as essential for one's prayer life. People lived in a Chris-

tian world and culture which was reflected in their laws, customs, amusements, and their very outlook on life. This situation has radically altered in the last two hundred years, and men must now compensate for this deficit through other media, principally reading. And as the de-Christianization of our world continues, the necessity for spiritual reading simultaneously increases. We stand in need of something to bridge the gap between our pagan surroundings and our conversation with Christ—spiritual reading fills this need.

There is today in our country an alarming decline in general reading of all types. It has been estimated that in 1955 an astonishing forty-eight percent of the American adult population reads *no books at all*, and only eighteen percent read from one to four books. The decline in reading is naturally reflected in religious reading as well. And, while the lack of secular reading will occasion a decrease in culture life, the decline in religious reading will have repercussions of a more serious nature—severe detriment to one's spiritual life. Any serious attempt to better one's life spiritually should, therefore, include the resolution to engage in more spiritual reading.

If we confine our reading to non-Catholic books, magazines and newspapers, we almost automatically exclude ourselves from full development in our prayer life. The maxims and philosophy of life expressed in these avenues of communication slowly begin to seep into our lives until eventually they occupy a ruling position. We will not have surrounded ourselves with a new climate; rather, the non-Catholic climate will have engulfed us (Chapter 19).

As this decry of the "de-Christianization of our world" was written in 1956, one can safely surmise that the necessity of cultivating the habit of spiritual reading can only have grown in the past several decades.

Spiritual Read-Aloud

As supported above, spiritual reading is an essential element of every Christian's life. However, as demonstrated by the ancient practice of spiritual read-aloud within monasteries, this habit is a powerful tool for shared community growth in the spiritual life. For Catholic families, the practice of reading spiritual books aloud produces four desirable effects:

I. It reinforces the habit of spiritual reading for each member of the family and allows each member to practice this habit regardless of age.

II. It reinforces the habit of spiritual conversation if the reading results in even a general discussion of the values and virtues being portrayed in the story.

III. It strengthens the family as the domestic Church where members exist to learn and live the Faith together for the support and enrichment of all family members.

IV. It allows the discussion and demonstration of the practical application of the Faith for all age levels.

The Habit of Spiritual Reading

As outlined above, establishing the habit of daily spiritual reading is essential to our spiritual growth. Through read-aloud, children can be taught at an early age that daily spiritual reading is a fun, rewarding exercise. Do make this time together pleasant by allowing the children to do crafts, draw, play quietly with puzzles, toys, etc. As long as their attention is not divided and they can participate in a discussion of the reading afterwards, allow quiet activity. One cannot expect children to sit piously with hands clasped prayerfully throughout the read-aloud session! As the children get older, encourage them to read other spiritual books, including the Bible, during a quiet time of their own.

Model this habit by allowing them to observe your habit of daily spiritual reading as well. Although the family read-aloud sessions may be as long as thirty minutes, private spiritual reading times may be considerably shorter depending on the habits and temperament of each child.

The Habit of Spiritual Conversation

The habit of spiritual conversation, for many families, begins with spiritual read-aloud. When each member of the family participates in a spiritual discussion of a religious book, the practice of discussing matters of faith and Christlike living begins to form. If the formation of holy habits and imitation of the saints is the goal, these discussions will become commonplace in the home as each member checks the others on their actions and words. As family members become more comfortable and open about spiritual matters, this practice will soon spread into other areas of their lives. Spiritual discussions with friends and other relatives will become more natural and in fact increase in importance. Sharing one's own spirituality, encouraging others, and accepting spiritual counsel will then become an inte-gral pattern of living.

Strengthening the Domestic Church

As we read more about the saints and their lives and begin to share our faith more openly with others, we realize the importance of holy companionship—living with others who share our faith ideas and supporting each other in our attempts to become more like Christ. Families begin to grow together in their knowledge of the Catholic faith and become more willing to support each other throughout the difficulties of community living. We begin to "bear one another's burdens with peace and harmony and unselfishness." Just as Christ has His Church to help bring salvation to all, we—as family members—have each other to provide mutual support and encouragement in our efforts to enter the narrow gate.

The Practical Application of the Faith
When lives of the saints are read aloud in the family setting, all aged children can participate in a discussion of the imitation of the saints' virtues and holy habits. Each member can help others understand how to apply the lessons the saints teach us on a practical level. All family members can help choose a particular habit or virtue upon which to focus. A reward system can be established for virtuous behavior. A family "plan of attack" on non-virtuous habits and attitudes can be developed, implemented, checked, and revised. All members can be encouraged and taught how to imitate Christ by the imitation of His saints.

Summary
Regular family read-aloud sessions that center around the lives of the saints and Christ-like living will benefit the family with an increased interest in reading—especially saintly literature—a growth in vocabulary, and an improved sense of family unity. Additionally, family members will be encouraged to develop the habit of spiritual reading on their own, will become more comfortable and experienced with spiritual conversation, and be able to apply the Truths of the Catholic faith on a practical level to all aspects of their lives—no matter what their age. The customs, habits, and attitudes of the family will grow to reflect those of an authentically Catholic culture. Perseverance in this simple daily ritual will help to "bridge the gap between our pagan surroundings and our conversation with Christ."

Janet P. McKenzie

When Mother Reads Aloud

When Mother reads aloud the past
Seems real as every day;
I hear the tramp of armies vast,
I see the spears and lances cast,
I join the thrilling fray;
Brave knights and ladies fair and proud
I meet when Mother reads aloud.

When Mother reads aloud, far lands
Seem very near and true;
I cross the desert's gleaming sands,
Or hunt the jungle's prowling bands,
Or sail the ocean blue;
Far heights, whose peaks the cold mists shroud,
I scale, when Mother reads aloud.

When Mother reads aloud I long
For noble deeds to do—
To help the right, redress the wrong,
It seems so easy to be strong, so simple to be true,
O, thick and fast the visions crowd
When Mother reads aloud.

−Anonymous

The Reading Mother

I had a mother who read to me
Sagas of pirates who scoured the sea,
Cutlasses clenched in their yellow teeth,
"Blackbirds" stowed in the hold beneath.

I had a mother who read me plays
Of ancient and gallant and golden days
Stories of Marmion and Ivanhoe,
Which every boy has a right to know.

I had a mother who read me tales
Of Gelert the hound of the hills of Wales,
True to his trust till his tragic death,
Faithfulness blest with his final breath.

I had a mother who read me things
That wholesome life to the boy-heart brings—
Stories that stir with an upward touch,
O, that each mother of boys were such.

You may have tangible wealth untold,
Caskets of jewels and coffers of gold.
Richer than I you can never be—
I had a mother who read to me.

–Strickland Gullilan

The Bridge of Life

Yon line of light across the sea,
That 'twist the em'rald shadows lies,
A bridge of silver seems to be,
Let down from rifts in cloudy skies.

Outstretching to the crystal rim,
Where meet and part the sails of snow,
It sparkles through the distance dim,
A pier where angels come and go.

Ah! thus, my soul, across Life's sea,
'Mid dark'ning shades of grief and care,
Outstretches to Eternity
The pure, resplendent Bridge of Prayer.

Time's airy ships advance, retreat—
This firm bridge leads to the skies—
For, following fast on angels' feet,
We pass from Prayer to Paradise!

—Eleanor C. Donnelly

How to Use This Study Guide

The King of the Golden City, An Allegory for Children, originally published in 1921, was written by Mother Mary Loyola of the Bar Convent in York, England, in response to a student's request for instructions along with "little stories" to help her prepare for First Holy Communion. An allegory is a story or narrative in which a moral principle or truth is presented by use of fictional characters or events. In an allegory characters, objects, and events usually symbolize, or parallel, something else. By figuring out what they symbolize or parallel, the lesson the story is intended to teach can be determined. Jesus often taught moral lessons by making using of parables; a parable is similar to an allegory except parables are not usually as symbolic in meaning. If desired, older students can study the parables of Jesus along with the study of *The King of the Golden City*.

It is highly recommended that this book be read orally with all family members together. Children may take turns reading, or a parent may read each day. Another option is to obtain the beautiful audio recording of this book by Catholic singer-songwriter Simonetta. It is available from The Saint Philomena Foundation, 15774 S. La Grange Road, Suite 140, Orland Park, IL 60462 or request a copy online at www.saintphilomena.com ("CDs and More – Free").

Narration

Each chapter should be narrated immediately after its oral reading. As emphasized by the British educator Charlotte Mason, narration is an important learning tool as it encourages children to listen attentively, increases comprehension, and teaches the art of storytelling. After the oral reading, children—beginning with the youngest—should be asked to narrate or tell back the story in their own words. Older students should then add further details to the first narration.

⇅ Parallel Figures Chart

After the day's reading and narration are complete, characters, objects, and events should be entered onto a large chart. This chart will list—from the beginning of the book until the end—important characters, objects, and events in one column and what each of these symbolizes, or parallels, in the next column. Be open to characters or objects symbolizing more than one thing or person. Perhaps it may seem to parallel one thing but as more information is gathered, it more likely parallels something different. This project should be completed as a family project. Characters, objects, and events to be deciphered are listed for each chapter. Some possible parallels for each character, object and event are included in the answer key. Attentive listeners will find more objects or persons to include. These may be entered onto a homemade chart or on the chart provided on page 75 below.

✓ Checking the Catechism

For each chapter, several words or doctrines of faith are listed. This will serve not only as a review of the catechism but also as an illustration of their practical application. It is recommended that either the *Saint Joseph Baltimore Catechism* or the *Catechism of the Catholic Church* be used as a reference. An attempt should also be made to locate the word or doctrine within the text of *The King of the Golden City*. Determine why that particular word or article of faith is an appropriate study for this chapter.

🏠 Discussion Topics

Use these suggestions for group discussion topics to review and expand the material with the student(s).

📖 Searching Scripture

As Catholics, we are sometimes accused of not knowing the Bible well. These citations are to encourage Bible reading and to increase the student's familiarity with Sacred Scripture. Passages from both the Old and New Testament books are utilized to help the student become familiar with the location of the various books of the Bible. Read these verses together; again try to determine why each passage was chosen by finding corresponding passages or ideas within the text of the particular chapter of *The King of the Golden City*. This is a good time to begin memorization of suitable Bible verses. Learn to relate God's Word to life's events and decisions.

✝ Growing in Holiness

To increase our understanding of God's love for us and His expectations for us without applying it to our daily lives is like casting seed upon rocks or into thorns. Read the parable of the sower in Matthew 13:1-23. Reflect on what it means to be chosen children of God. Ask what fruit we can bear from reading and analyzing *The King of the Golden City*. Begin to live God's Word.

" " Carmelite Connections

For those interested in deepening their prayer life, this section provides quotations from three Carmelite saints: St. Teresa of Avila, St. John of the Cross, and St. Therese of the Child Jesus. These quotations provide helpful comments on the transformation of the little maid as she deepens her friendship with the King and progresses in heroic virtue and spiritual perfection. Older siblings and adults can profit from the teachings of the Carmelite saints regarding our relationship with God as well as the stages and methods of deep Carmelite prayer. Allow these saints to assist you in understanding God's love and desire for us, the obstacles to an

intimate relationship with Him, and how to make true progress toward perfect union with our Lord and King.

If desired, read with the older children the parable(s) of
Jesus that coordinate with of each chapter of *The King of the
Golden City* as outlined on pages 77-79 of this study guide.

The King of the Golden City

Golden City

Study Guide

Chapter 1
The Meeting in the Wood

Narration
After the oral reading of this chapter is complete, take turns narrating the events of this chapter.

Parallel Figures Chart
the King
the country of the travelers (Land of Exile)
the Golden City
the rebel lord Malignus
the Happy Ones
the maid
the maid's hut
the wildflowers
the King's simple robe of white
the path to the hut
the quarter of an hour spent within the hut together
the unclean hut
no fit spot to lay them (King's gifts) down
the wounds of the King

✓ Checking the Catechism
heaven   grace
devil   penance

Discussion Topics
1. Compare the relationship between the little maid and Jesus when they were meeting in the woods with their relationship after Jesus had come to her hut. What was

1

different when she began to take His coming for granted?

2. Why is it important to always prepare ourselves for His
communion with us? How can the idea of the decoration
of flowers in anticipation of His coming help us? (The
symbolism of the different flowers as they relate to the
different virtues is demonstrated well in *The Catholic
Girl's Guide* by Rev. Francis X. Lasance—as well as the
*Little Flowers General Guide and Manual (Little Flow-
ers Girls Club)*.

Searching Scripture
Matthew 11:28-30
Hebrews 11:13-16
Hebrews 13:14

Growing in Holiness
Adequately prepare for Jesus' coming to you in each Holy
Communion. Never take this great Gift for granted! Be aware
of distractions during both your preparation and your thanksgiving time. Be sure to spend time after each Communion
in thanksgiving. Note that when Jesus comes to the little
maid in her hut, He stays with her for a quarter of an hour.
The Church teaches that the physical presence of Jesus remains with each of us for ten to twenty minutes before the
Host is completely ingested into our bodies. Be aware of
His physical presence when you receive Him in Holy Communion. Use this time for thanksgiving and prayer.

Carmelite Connections
1. ". . . mental prayer, in my view, is nothing but friendly
intercourse, and frequent solitary converse, with Him
Who we know loves us." (*Life of the Holy Mother Teresa
of Jesus* VIII.5)

2. "A fine humility it would be if I had the Emperor of Heaven and earth in my house, coming to it to do me a favour and to delight in my company, and I were so humble that I would not answer His questions, nor remain with Him, nor accept what He gave me, but left Him alone." (*Way of Perfection* XXVIII.3)
3. "The only way I have of proving my love is to strew flowers before Thee—that is to say, I will let no tiny sacrifice pass, no look, no word. I wish to profit by the smallest actions, and to do them for Love. I wish to suffer for Love's sake, and for Love's sake even to rejoice: thus shall I strew flowers. Not one shall I find without scattering its petals before Thee . . ." (*Story of a Soul*, Chapter XI)
4. ". . . until the accidents of bread have been consumed by our natural heat, the good Jesus is with us and we should not lose so good an opportunity but should come to Him. If, while He went about in the world, the sick were healed merely by touching His clothes, how can we doubt that He will work miracles when He is within us, if we have faith, or that He will give us what we ask of Him since he is in our house? His Majesty is not wont to offer us too little payment for His lodging if we treat Him well." (*Way of Perfection* XXXIV.9)
5. "Imagine that this Lord Himself is at your side and see how lovingly and how humbly He is teaching you—and, believe me, you should stay with so good a Friend for as long as you can before you leave Him. If you become accustomed to having Him at your side, and if He sees that you love Him to be there and are always trying to please Him, you will never be able, as we put it, to send Him away, nor will He ever fail you. He will help you in all your trials; you will have Him everywhere. Do you think it is a small thing to have such a Friend as that beside you?" (*Way of Perfection* XXVI.1)

6. "If I had understood then, as I do now, how this great King *really* dwells within this little palace of my soul, I should not have left Him alone so often, but should have stayed with Him and never have allowed His dwelling-place to get so dirty. How wonderful it is that He, Whose greatness could fill a thousand worlds, and very many more, should confine Himself within so small a space." (*Way of Perfection* XXVIII.12)

As we first come to know the little maid, she is just beginning her journey toward the Golden City. She shows us some characteristics of the classical first stage of perfection in the Christian life—the purgative way: a growing desire to travel the road toward perfection, the continual struggle against sin and temptation, increased interest in prayer, and the longing to atone for past sins.

Chapter 2
The Little Maid Finds She Must Help in Her Training

Narration

After the oral reading of this chapter is complete, take turns narrating the events of this chapter.

Parallel Figures Chart

lieutenants
prince of the Court (Prince Guardian)
teachers

Checking the Catechism

redemption
the Ten Commandments
the happiness of heaven
obedience

Discussion Topics

1. What must we do to be crowned by Jesus in death?
2. Why does Jesus provide us with other teachers rather than always teaching and leading us Himself? Is it easier to obey Jesus directly or His teachers? Why?
3. What has the King done to make our union with Him in the Golden City easier?

Searching Scripture

Exodus 20:1-17
Isaiah 30:20-21
John 14:15
1 Corinthians 9:24-27

✠ Growing in Holiness

Those in authority over you are representatives of Jesus Himself. Treat the direction and instruction received from priests and your parents as coming directly from Jesus.

❝❞ Carmelite Connections

1. "Our Lord has no need of books or teachers to instruct our souls. He, the Teacher of Teachers, instructs us without any noise of words. I have never heard Him speak, yet I know He is within me. He is there, always guiding and inspiring me; and just when I need them, lights, hitherto unseen, break in." (*Story of a Soul*, Chapter VIII)

2. "Humility must always be doing its work like the bee making its honey in the hive; without humility all will be lost. Still, we should remember that the bee is constantly flying about from flower to flower, and in the same way, believe me, the soul must sometimes emerge from self-knowledge and soar aloft in meditation upon the greatness and the majesty of its God. Doing this will help it to realize its own baseness better than thinking of its own nature, and it will be freer from the reptiles which enter the first rooms—that is, the rooms of self-knowledge. For although, as I say, it is through the abundant mercy of God that the soul studies to know itself, yet one can have too much of a good thing, as the saying goes, and believe me, we shall reach much greater heights of virtue by thinking upon the virtue of God than if we stay in our own little plot of ground and tie ourselves down to it completely." (*Interior Castle* I.ii.8)

Dilecta continues to proceed through the purgative way of perfection. When we compare Dilecta's present condition with the traits of St. Teresa of Avila's seven mansions, we see that she has entered the castle through prayer and has several characteristics of the first mansions: an earnest, continual effort to avoid sin; a desire to avoid offending God; and imperfect progress due to her attachment to self and her desires. She is still absorbed in worldly matters but is beginning to turn from the worldly life to a life centered on the Trinity.

Holy Scripture speaks of this first Teresian mansion in Titus 2:11-14: "For the grace of God has appeared, saving all and training us to reject godless ways and worldly desires and to live temperately, justly, and devoutly in this age, as we await the blessed hope, the appearance of the glory of the great God and of our savior Jesus Christ, who gave Himself for us to deliver us from all lawlessness and to cleanse for himself a people as his own, eager to do what is good."

Chapter 3
The King's Laws

Narration
After the oral reading of this chapter is complete, take turns narrating the events of this chapter.

Parallel Figures Chart
signs
the straight road

✓ Checking the Catechism
temptation
free will (will)

Discussion Topics
1. What is the purpose of the commandments of God, the laws of the Church, the ideals of the Beatitudes and examples of the saints? Why are we happier when we are obedient to them?
2. Why are we happier when we submit ourselves to the example of Christ and fight our own natural tendency toward sin? What has God given us to make this battle against our own wills easier?

Searching Scripture
Psalm 84
Isaiah 35:8-10
1 Peter 2:11

✝ Growing in Holiness

Practice saying "no" to yourself by making little sacrifices each day in order to strengthen your will. Every day do at least one thing that you do not want to do. Always remember that you are on a journey; life here on earth is temporary. Our real home is not here but in heaven. In order to obtain heaven, we must imitate Jesus in all things including the carrying of the Cross.

" " Carmelite Connections

1. "With regard to these first Mansions. . .we are tricked by all kinds of deceptions. The devil is less successful with those who are nearer the King's dwelling-place; but at this early stage, as the soul is still absorbed in worldly affairs, engulfed in worldly pleasure and puffed up with worldly honours and ambitions, its vassals, which are the senses and the faculties. . .have not the same power, and such a soul is easily vanquished, although it may desire not to offend God and may perform good works." (*Interior Castle* I.ii.12)
2. "This seems to me to be the condition of a soul which, though not in a bad state, is so completely absorbed in things of the world and so deeply immersed, as I have said, in possessions or honours or business, that, although as a matter of fact it would like to gaze at the castle and enjoy its beauty, it is prevented from doing so, and seems quite unable to free itself from all these impediments. Everyone, however, who wishes to enter the second Mansions, will be well advised, as far as his state of life permits, to try to put aside all unnecessary affairs and business." (*Interior Castle* I.ii.14)
3. ". . . if we are to acquire increasing merit, and not, like Saul and Judas, to be lost, our only possible safety consists in obedience and in never swerving from the law of God; I

am referring to those to whom He grants these favors, and in fact to all." (*Interior Castle* V.iii.2)

4. "If you are willing to bear in peace the trial of not being pleased with yourself, you will be offering the Divine Master a home in your heart. It is true that you will suffer, because you will be like a stranger to your own house; but do not be afraid—the poorer you are, the more Jesus will love you. I know that He is better pleased to see you stumbling in the night upon a stony road, than walking in the full light of day upon a path carpeted with flowers, because these flowers might hinder your advance." (St. Therese of the Child Jesus in a letter to her sister Celine dated March 12, 1899)

5. "She [St. Therese of the Child Jesus] is a very intelligent child, but has not nearly so sweet a disposition as her sister, and her stubbornness is almost unconquerable. When she has said 'No,' nothing will make her change." (*Story of a Soul*, Chapter I)

6. "Oh . . . how little one should think about resting, and how little one should care about honours, and how far one ought to be from wishing to be esteemed in the very least if the Lord makes His special abode in the soul. For if the soul is much with Him, as it is right it should be, it will very seldom think of itself; its whole thought will be concentrated upon finding ways to please Him and upon showing Him how it loves Him. This . . . is the aim of prayer . . ." (*Interior Castle* VII.iv.6)

Although still proceeding through the purgative way and the first mansions, Dilecta is beginning to exhibit some of the characteristics of the Teresian second mansion: a beginning awareness of the conflict between self-will and the divine call, and an increased willingness to embrace sacrifice in order to please Jesus. Matthew's Gospel addresses the matter of doing God's will by quoting Jesus' description of a true disciple, "Not everyone who says to me, 'Lord, Lord,' will enter the kingdom of heaven, but only the one who does the will of my Father in heaven." (7:21) (The purgative way corresponds to the first three Teresian mansions.)

Chapter 4—The King's Household

Narration
After the oral reading of this chapter is complete, take turns narrating the events of this chapter.

Parallel Figures Chart
a large House   the Hospital or Infirmary
the School   the Banquet Hall
the Gymnasium   the Royal Audience Chamber
the Armory

✓ Checking the Catechism
the Church   the sacraments

Discussion Topics
1. Outline each of the seven sacraments stating the purpose each performs in helping us on our journey toward heaven. Is one more important than the others? If so, which one?
2. Other than the sacraments, what else has God provided to assist us in obtaining our heavenly reward?

Searching Scripture
John 14:2
Romans 8:14-17
1 Corinthians 2:9

Growing in Holiness
Make generous use of God's gift of the sacraments in order to strengthen your will. Receive the Sacraments of Reconciliation and the Eucharist as often as possible.

🗨 **Carmelite Connections**

1. "O Jesus, my Divine Spouse, grant that my baptismal robe may never be sullied. Take me from this world rather than let me stain my soul by committing the least wilful fault. May I never seek or find aught but Thee alone!" (*Story of a Soul*, Chapter VIII)

2. "Open, O Jesus, the Book of Life, in which are written the deeds of Thy Saints: all the deeds told in that book I long to have accomplished for Thee." (*Story of a Soul*, Chapter XI)

3. "If we do not give ourselves to His majesty as resolutely as He gives Himself to us, He will be doing more than enough for us if He leaves us in mental prayer and from time to time visits us as He would visit servants in His vineyard. But these others are His beloved children, whom He would never want to banish from His side; and, as they have no desire to leave Him, He never does so. He seats them at His table, and feeds them with His own food . . ." (*Way of Perfection* XVI.9)

4. "We are like soldiers who, however long they have served, must always be ready for their captain to send them away on any duty which he wants to entrust to them, since it is he who is paying them. And how much better is the payment given by our King than by people on this earth!" (*Way of Perfection* XVIII.3)

5. "As the warriors of old trained their children in the profession of arms, so [Marie] trained me for the battle of life, and roused my ardour by pointing to the victor's glorious palm. She spoke, too, of the imperishable riches which are so easy to amass each day, and of the folly of trampling them under foot when one has but to stoop and gather them. When she talked so eloquently, I was sorry that I was the only one to listen to her teaching, for, in my simplicity, it seemed to me that the greatest sinners would be converted if they but heard her, and that,

forsaking the perishable riches of this world, they would seek none but the riches of Heaven." (*Story of a Soul,* Chapter IV)

6. "Each time that my enemy would provoke me to combat, I behave as a gallant soldier. I know that a duel is an act of cowardice, and so, without once looking him in the face, I turn my back on the foe, then I hasten to my Saviour . . ." (*Story of a Soul,* Chapter IX)

7. ". . . this person, though by no means perfect, always tried to strengthen her faith, when she communicated, by thinking that it was exactly as if she saw the Lord entering her house, with her own bodily eyes, for she believed in very truth that this Lord was entering her abode, and she ceased, as far as she could, to think of outward things, and went into her abode with Him. She tried to recollect her senses so that they might all become aware of this great blessing, or rather, so that they should not hinder the soul from becoming conscious of it." (*Way of Perfection* XXXIV.8)

8. ". . . It [the soul preparing itself for union with God] begins to utilize the general help which God gives to us all, and to make use of the remedies which He left in His Church—such as frequent confessions, good books, and sermons, for these are the remedies for a soul, dead in negligences and sins and frequently plunged into temptation. The soul begins to live and nourishes itself on this food, and on good meditations, until it is full grown." (*Interior Castle* V.ii.4)

Chapter 5
A Troublesome Partner

Narration
After the oral reading of this chapter is complete, take turns narrating the events of this chapter.

Parallel Figures Chart
Self   lamp of "Peace"

✓ Checking the Catechism
actual sin
punishment of Adam
anger
theological virtues (virtues)

Discussion Topics
1. Mother Loyola refers to the "lamp of Peace." What exactly is the lamp to which she refers? Discuss ways to keep your lamp burning. What types of thoughts, words, or actions dim your lamp or allow it to go out?
2. Do you rely more on Self or your Prince Guardian to help you make decisions? In what ways are you allowing Self to dictate to you? Remember to listen to your Prince Guardian. Ask him/her to help you remain in the state of grace so that your name continues to be written in the Book of Life.

Searching Scripture
2 Samuel 22:29
Job 18:5-6
Job 21:17
Matthew 5:15-16

✝ Growing in Holiness

Develop a plan to help keep not only your lamp but also the lamp of each member of your family burning brightly. What habits or temperaments will need to be eliminated in order to accomplish this? Does your interaction with others need to change in order not to dim their lamps? Learn from Dilecta's Prince Guardian: Do not try to correct all your faults at once. What can you do to gain strength to persevere in your plan?

" " Carmelite Connections

1. In discussing the importance of self-knowledge in the first mansions, St. Teresa of Avila states, ". . . self-knowledge is so important that, even if you were raised right up to the heavens, I should like you never to relax your cultivation of it; so long as we are on this earth, nothing matters more to us than humility. And so I repeat that it is a very good thing—excellent, indeed—to begin by entering the room where humility is acquired rather than by flying off to the other rooms. For that is the way to make progress, and, if we have a safe, level road to walk along, why should we desire wings to fly? Let us rather try to get the greatest possible profit out of walking. As I see it, we shall never succeed in knowing ourselves unless we seek to know God . . ." (*Interior Castle* I.ii.9)

2. In regards to traits of the second mansion, St. Teresa says, "The will shows the soul how this true Lover never leaves it, but goes with it everywhere and gives it life and being. Then the understanding comes forward and makes the soul realize that, for however many years it may live, it can never hope to have a better friend, for the world is full of falsehood and these pleasures which the devil pictures to it are accompanied by trials and cares and annoyances; and tells it to be certain that out-

side this castle it will find neither security nor peace: let it refrain from visiting one house after another when its own house is full of good things, if it will only enjoy them. How fortunate it is to be able to find all that it needs, as it were, at home, especially when it has a Host Who will put all good things into its possession, unless, like the Prodigal Son, it desires to go astray and eat the food of the swine!" (*Interior Castle* II.i.5)

3. "All that the beginner in prayer has to do—and you must not forget this, for it is very important—is to labour and be resolute and prepare himself with all possible diligence to bring his will into conformity with the will of God. . . . you may be quite sure that this comprises the very greatest perfection which can be attained on the spiritual road. The more perfectly a person practices it, the more he will receive of the Lord and the greater the progress he will make on this road." (*Interior Castle* II.i.9)

4. "There is no other remedy for this evil [giving up prayer] . . . except to start again at the beginning; otherwise the soul will keep on losing a little more every day—please God that it may come to realize this." (*Interior Castle* II.i.11)

5. "May it please His Majesty to grant us to understand how much we cost Him, that the servant is not greater than his Lord, that we must . . . work if we would enjoy His glory, and for that reason we must perforce pray, lest we enter continually into temptation." (*Interior Castle* II.i.12)

6. ". . . My soul was yet far from mature, and I had to pass through many trials before reaching the haven of peace, before tasting the delicious fruits of perfect love and of complete abandonment to God's Will." (*Story of a Soul*, Chapter III)

7. ". . . Her lamp, filled to the brim with the oil of virtue, burned brightly to the end." (*Story of a Soul*, Epilogue)

Dilecta begins to show more traits of the Teresian second mansions in that she is beginning to learn virtue, she continues to conform her will to the will of God, and she is starting to cheerfully begin again after falling.

Chapter 6
The King's Table

Narration
After the oral reading of this chapter is complete, take turns narrating the events of this chapter.

Parallel Figures Chart
daily banquet
the white robe
ante-chamber
small stains on the white robe
the jewels with which the King adorned the white robe

✓ Checking the Catechism
Holy Communion
sacrilege
confession

Discussion Topics
Discuss the advantages and possible pitfalls of receiving Holy Communion as early as the age of seven as well as receiving Jesus on a daily basis rather than once or twice a month—or only on special feast days. (The regulations regarding the reception of Holy Communion were changed only a few years before *The King of the Golden City* was written.) Why do you think these laws of the Church were revised?

Searching Scripture
Song of Songs 2:4
Matthew 22:1-14
Luke 14:12-14

✝ Growing in Holiness

Begin to look at Mass as a banquet feast. "Give us today our daily bread" (Matthew 6:11). "Jesus said to them, 'My food is to do the will of the one who sent me and to finish his work'" (John 4:34). "For my flesh is true food, and my blood is true drink" (John 6:55). Recall that several saints have lived exclusively on the Holy Eucharist. Allow the Bread of Life to fill your spiritual hunger. Try to receive this Food daily.

❝❞ Carmelite Connections

1. "For unless we want to be foolish and to close our minds to facts, we cannot suppose that this is the work of the imagination, as it is when we think of the Lord on the Cross, or of other incidents of the Passion, and picture within ourselves how these things happened. This [receiving Jesus in the Most Blessed Sacrament] is something which is happening now; it is absolutely true; and we have no need to go and seek Him somewhere a long way off." (*Way of Perfection* XXXIV.9)

2. "Beneath those accidents of bread, we can approach Him; for, if the King disguises Himself, it would seem that we need not mind coming to Him without so much circumspection and ceremony: by disguising Himself, He has, as it were, obliged Himself to submit to this. Who, otherwise, would dare approach Him so unworthily, with so many imperfections and with such lukewarm zeal?" (*Way of Perfection* XXXIV.10)

3. "Oh, we know not what we ask! How much better does his Wisdom know what we need! He reveals Himself to those who He knows will profit by His presence; though unseen by bodily eyes, He has many ways of revealing Himself to the soul through deep inward emotions and

by various other means. Delight to remain with Him; do not lose such an excellent time for talking with Him as the hour after Communion. *Remember that this is a very profitable hour for the soul.*" (*Way of Perfection* XXXIV.11)

4. ". . . We need no wings to go in search of Him but have only to find a place where we can be alone and look upon Him present within us. Nor need we feel strange in the presence of so kind a Guest; we must talk to Him very humbly, as we should to our father, ask Him for things as we should ask a father, tell Him our troubles, beg Him to put them right, and yet realize that we are not worthy to be called His children." (*Way of Perfection* XXVIII.2)

5. "But if we pay no heed to Him save when we have received Him, and go away from Him in search of other and baser things, what can He do? Will He have to drag us by force to look at Him *and be with Him* because He desires to reveal Himself to us? No; for when He revealed himself to all men plainly, and told them clearly who He was, they did not treat Him at all well—very few of them, indeed, even believed Him. So He grants us an exceedingly great favour when He is pleased to show us that it is He Who is in the Most Holy Sacrament. But He will not reveal Himself openly and communicate His glories and bestow His treasure save on those who He knows greatly desire Him, for these are His true friends." (*Way of Perfection* XXXIV.14)

Chapter 7
Dilecta Asks for a Change

Narration
After the oral reading of this chapter is complete, take turns narrating the events of this chapter.

Parallel Figures Chart
Bridget

✓ Checking the Catechism
Two Great Commandments   hope
conscience   virtue

Discussion Topics
1. Discuss the importance of controlling your free will.
2. How can a well-trained conscience help us in this life's journey?

Searching Scripture
Matthew 7:12
Read the famous words of Job in Job 1:21-22. ("Job's comforter" refers to one of the three friends of Job who, in consoling him, tried to get him to acknowledge sin, do penance, and submit to God as they believed his suffering was due to his sin.)

Growing in Holiness
Choose a virtue such as patience, perseverance, charity, etc., and practice it every day by saying "no" to yourself and your own inclination to sin. Ask each morning for your Prince Guardian's help in conquering your Self; resolve at various

times throughout the day to renew this vow through prayer. Each night examine your conscience regarding your words, thoughts, actions, and omissions of that day relative to that virtue. Thank God for His help in your progress, and acknowledge your failures with an Act of Contrition. Work on this one virtue for at least two weeks before choosing another.

❝❞ Carmelite Connections

1. "Why, then, do we shrink from interior mortification, since this is the means by which every other kind of mortification may become much more meritorious and perfect, so that it can then be practised with greater tranquility and ease? This, as I have said, is acquired by gradual progress and by never indulging our own will and desire, even in small things, until we have succeeded in subduing the body to the spirit." (*Way of Perfection* XII.1)

2. "It is absurd to think that we can enter Heaven without first entering our own souls—without getting to know ourselves, and reflecting on the wretchedness of our nature and what we owe to God, and continually imploring His mercy. . . . If we never look at Him or think of what we owe Him, and of the death which He suffered for our sakes, I do not see how we can get to know Him or do good works in His service. For what can be the value of faith without works, or of works which are not united with the merits of our Lord Jesus Christ? And what but such thoughts can arouse us to love this Lord?" (*Interior Castle* II.i.12)

Chapter 8
The King's Armory

Narration

After the oral reading of this chapter is complete, take turns narrating the events of this chapter.

Parallel Figures Chart

soldiers of the Royal Army
enrolled in my Army
Jolly Ones or Triflers

✓ **Checking the Catechism**

faith
prayer
Confirmation
indelible mark of Confirmation

Discussion Topics

1. Describe how we are to fight for Christ. What weapons are we to use? Are we expected to fight in open warfare each day? What weapons are to be used each day in fulfilling our daily duty?
2. What more than anything else brings us to victory and reward?

Searching Scripture

Matthew 6:19-21
Luke 6:43-45
Ephesians 6:11-17

✠ Growing in Holiness

Meditate each morning, if only for a few minutes, before the crucifix. Reminding ourselves frequently of the great sacrifice of love that Jesus made for us can help to keep our priorities correctly ordered. Think often of the length of eternity compared to our span of life on this earth. Keep focused on the importance of pleasing the One who created you, so you may spend all of eternity in His Presence.

66 99 Carmelite Connections

1. "What a strange thing! You might suppose that the devil never tempted those who do not walk along the road of prayer!" (*Way of Perfection* XXXIX.7)
2. ". . . Wherever the king is, or so they say, the court is too; that is to say, wherever God is, there is Heaven. No doubt, you can believe that in any place where His Majesty is, there is fullness of glory. Remember how St. Augustine tells us about his seeking God in many places and eventually finding Him within himself." (*Way of Perfection* XXVIII.2)

Chapter 9
The King's Infirmary

Narration

After the oral reading of this chapter is complete, take turns narrating the events of this chapter.

Parallel Figures Chart

wounded soldiers   sullied white robe

Checking the Catechism

mortal sin
venial sin
how to keep from committing sin

Discussion Topics

God provides for all our needs. But we may not always make use of the opportunities for increased grace that He offers us. Discuss the main reasons many commit sin. How can you apply this knowledge to ensure victory in the fight?

Searching Scripture

Matthew 7: 7-11   Luke 11:3

Growing in Holiness

Each day ask for the graces you need to fight your sinful habits and to avoid occasions of sin. If you are not able to receive Communion daily, be sure to make a spiritual communion often during the day—especially in times of temptation or when tired.

〝〞 Carmelite Connections

1. "Show us then, O our good Master, some way in which we may live through this most dangerous warfare without frequent surprise. The best way we can do this . . . is to use the love and fear given us by His Majesty. For love will make us quicken our steps, while fear will make us look where we are setting our feet so that we shall not fall on the road where there are so many obstacles. Along that road all living creatures must pass, and if we have these two things we shall certainly not be deceived." (*Way of Perfection* XL.1)

2. "Keep this in mind, for it is very important advice, so do not neglect it until you find you have such a fixed determination not to offend the Lord that you would rather lose a thousand lives, *and be persecuted by the whole world*, than commit one mortal sin, and until you are most careful not to commit venial sins. I am referring now to sins committed knowingly: as far as those of the other kind are concerned, who can fail to commit these frequently? . . . From any sin, however small, committed with full knowledge, may God deliver us, especially since we are sinning against so great a Sovereign and realizing that He is watching us! . . . If we commit a sin in this way, however slight, it seems to me that our offence is not small but very, very great." (*Way of Perfection* XLI.5)

3. "He prays for nothing more than this 'today' since He has given us this most holy Bread. He has given it to us fo ever . . . as the sustenance and manna of humanity. We can have it whenever we please and we shall not die of hunger save through our own fault. . . *He teaches us to fix our desires upon heavenly things and to pray that we may begin to enjoy these things while here on earth.*" (*Way of Perfection* XXXIV.2)

4. "I have often observed that Our Lord will not give me any store of provisions, but nourishes me each moment with food that is ever new; I find it within me without knowing how it has come there. I simply believe that it is Jesus Himself hidden in my poor heart, who is secretly at work, inspiring me with what He wishes me to do as each occasion arises." (*Story of a Soul*, Chapter VIII)

5. ". . . The Lord says: 'Ask, and it shall be given you.' If you do not believe His Majesty in those passages of His Gospel where He gives us this assurance, it will be of little help to you . . . for me to weary my brains by telling you of it. Still, I will say to anyone who is in doubt that she will lose little by putting the matter to the test; for this journey has the advantage of giving us *very much* more than we ask or shall even get so far as to desire. This is a never-failing truth; I know it." (*Way of Perfection* XXIII.6)

The beginning stage of those striving for perfection—the purgative way—in which the struggle against temptation and sin is paramount is characterized in this chapter. Dilecta continues her journey toward the Golden City still within this first classical stage of perfection. Within the mansions of St. Teresa, Dilecta remains in the second mansion, typified by her desire to conform her will to God's will and her interest in using the tools God has provided to ward off temptation and remain in the state of grace.

Chapter 10
The Little Maid in an Idle Mood

Narration
After the oral reading of this chapter is complete, take turns narrating the events of this chapter.

Parallel Figures Chart
master of his own house   soft knock at the door

Checking the Catechism
remission of sin
merit
indulgence
reparation
temporal punishment

Discussion Topics
Why is it important to pay the debt we have incurred through our sins? What happens if we die with this debt unpaid? What does Jesus do to give us the opportunity to pay off this debt?

Searching Scripture
Sirach 33:28   Matthew 5:23-26

Growing in Holiness
Think of at least three practical things you can do to start making reparation for your sins and the sins of the whole world right now. Ask your guardian angel each day to help you not only to watch for opportunities to make reparation but also to make the best possible use of them.

66 99 Carmelite Connections

1. ". . . All of his [the devil's] powers are in the external sphere." (*Interior Castle* VI.ii.6)

2. "Remember that in few of the mansions of this castle are we free from struggles with devils. . . . In some of them, the wardens, who . . . are the faculties, have the strength for the fight; but . . . we should not cease to be watchful against the devil's wiles, lest he deceive us in the guise of an angel of light. For there are a multitude of ways in which he can deceive us, and gradually make his way into the castle, and until he is actually there we do not realize it." (*Interior Castle* I.ii.15)

3. "May His Majesty be pleased to grant us *to experience* this before He takes us from this life, for it will be a great thing at the hour of death, *when we are going we know not whither*, to realize that we shall be judged by One Whom we have loved above all things. . . . Once our debts have been paid we shall be able to walk in safety. We shall not be going into a foreign land, but into our own country, for it belongs to Him Whom we have loved so truly and Who Himself loves us. Remember . . . the greatness of the gain which comes from this love, and of our loss if we do not possess it, for in that case we shall be delivered into the hands of the tempter. . . ." (*Way of Perfection* XL.8)

4. "What a wonderful thing it is . . . to have a wise and prudent Master who foresees our perils. . . . No words could ever exaggerate the importance of this. The Lord, then, saw it was necessary to awaken such souls and to remind them that they have enemies, and how much greater danger they are in if they are unprepared. . . ." (*Way of Perfection* XXXVII.7)

Chapter 11
The Broad Road

Narration

After the oral reading of this chapter is complete, take turns narrating the events of this chapter.

Parallel Figures Chart

the fair   Daisy
the play   the broad road

✓ Checking the Catechism

Fourth Commandment
Sixth Commandment
saint
temptation

Discussion Topics

Daisy may be defined as one of the Jolly Ones—a Trifler. Oftentimes the pressure Christians receive from Triflers is hard to resist. Discuss the technique Dilecta uses. What else might she have done to resist Daisy and the other girls? What might you do when you are pressured by others to participate in something that may be sinful or harmful?

Searching Scripture

Psalm 95:7-9
Proverbs 1:8-15
Proverbs 4:10-27
Sirach 21:1-6
Matthew 7:13-14

✝ Growing in Holiness

Dilecta gives in to her Prince Guardian when she feels his prayers for her. Recite often the prayer to your guardian angel asking for his/her guidance and spiritual help. Remember the power of prayer. Pray often the Our Father—"Lead us not into temptation but deliver us from evil" and the Hail Mary—"Pray for us sinners now and at the hour of our death." Pray not only for yourself but also for others.

"" Carmelite Connections

1. "How often people stray through not taking advice, especially when there is a risk of doing someone harm!" (*Way of Perfection* IV.14)
2. "You already know that the first stone of this foundation must be a good conscience and that you must make every effort to free yourselves from even venial sins and follow the greatest possible perfection." (*Way of Perfection* V.3)
3. "A . . . reason why we must be resolute is that this will give the devil less opportunity to tempt us. He is very much afraid of resolute souls, knowing by experience that they inflict great injury upon him, and, when he plans to do them harm he only profits them and others and is himself the loser. We must not become unwatchful, or count upon this, for we have to do with treacherous folk, who are great cowards and dare not attack the wary, but, if they see we are careless, will work us great harm. And if they know anyone to be changeable, and not resolute in *doing* what is good and firmly determined to persevere, they will not leave him alone either by night or by day and will suggest to him endless misgivings and difficulties." (*Way of Perfection* XXIII.4)
4. ". . . for, if they lose their Guide, the good Jesus, they will be unable to find their way. . . ." (*Interior Castle* VI.vii.7)

5. ". . . as if we could arrive at these Mansions by letting others make the journey for us! That is not possible. . . . so, for the love of the Lord, let us make a real effort; let us leave our reason and fears in His hands and let us forget the weakness of our nature which is apt to cause us so much worry." (*Interior Castle* III.ii.9)

6. "Do not be dismayed . . . at the number of things which you have to consider before setting out on this Divine journey, which is the royal road to Heaven. By taking this road, we gain such precious treasures that it is no wonder if the cost seems to us a high one. The time will come when we shall realize that all we have paid has been nothing at all by comparison with the greatness of our prize. Let us now return to those who wish to travel on this road. . . . It is most important—all important, in-deed—that they should begin well by making an earnest and most determined resolve not to halt until they reach their goal . . . however hard they may have to labour. . . ." (*Way of Perfection* XXI.1-2)

7. "For it is as if He [Christ] had said: In truth the way is very strait, more so than you think. . . . He says first that the gate is strait, to make it clear that, in order for the soul to enter by this gate, which is Christ, and which comes at the beginning of the road, the will must first be straitened and detached in all things sensual and tem-poral, and God must be loved above them all. . . . For this path ascending the high mountain of perfection leads upward, and is narrow, and therefore requires trav-ellers that have no burden weighing upon them with re-spect to lower things, neither aught that embarrasses them with respect to higher things: God alone must be the object of our search and attainment." (*Ascent to Mount Carmel* II.VII.7)

8. "What a strange idea that one could ever expect to travel on a road infested by thieves, for the purpose of gaining some great treasure, without running into danger!

Worldly people like to take life peaceably; but they will deny themselves sleep, *perhaps* for nights on end, in order to gain a farthing's profit, and they will leave you no peace either of body or of soul. If, when you are on the way to gaining this treasure . . . and are travelling by this royal road—this safe road trodden by our King and by His elect and His saints—if even then they tell you it is full of danger and make you so afraid, what will be the dangers encountered by those who think they will be able to gain this treasure and yet are not on the road to it?" (*Way of Perfection* XXI.5)

9. " . . . Never pay heed to . . . matters of popular opinion. This is no time for believing everyone; believe only those whom you see modeling their lives on the life of Christ. Endeavour always to have a good conscience; practice humility; despise all worldly things; and believe firmly in the teaching of our Holy Mother Church. You may then be quite sure that you are on a [very] good road." (*Way of Perfection* XXI.10)

Dilecta continues through the second mansions by advancing in virtue, persevering in the battle against her will, and by being concerned about good companionship.

Chapter 12
The Fair

Narration

After the oral reading of this chapter is complete, take turns narrating the events of this chapter.

Parallel Figures Chart

bad sweets sprinkled with sugar
poisonous powders
Dark Valley

✓ Checking the Catechism

scruples (Use a Catholic dictionary.)
Second Commandment
happiness
temperance

Discussion Topics

What are some signs that the devil is near? How can we frighten him away?

Searching Scripture

Luke 4:36   2 Corinthians 2:11
Romans 16:19-20   Philippians 2:5-11

✝ Growing in Holiness

When tempted by the devil or aware of his influence and presence, rebuke him in the name of Jesus. Remember how cowardly he is when the name of Jesus is spoken. Memorize Psalm 124:8. Be sure to pray the Sign of the Cross whenever you hear the name of Jesus used as a curse or in blasphemy.

Unfortunately, this sin has become acceptable behavior by many in our society and is widely used in the media.

⟪ ⟫ Carmelite Connections

1. "Happily for me, I had visible guardian angels to guide me. . . . They chose books suitable to my age, which interested me and at the same time provided food for my thoughts and affections." (*Story of a Soul*, Chapter IV)

2. "But the devil comes with his artful wiles, and, under the colour of doing good, sets about undermining it in trivial ways, and involving it in practices which, so he gives it to understand, are not wrong; little by little he darkens its understanding, and weakens its will, and causes its self-love to increase, until in one way and another he begins to withdraw it from the love of God and to persuade it to indulge its own wishes." (*Interior Castle*, V.iv.7)

3. "Beware also . . . of certain kinds of humility which the devil inculcates in us and which make us very uneasy about the gravity of our *past sins*. There are many ways in which he is accustomed to depress us so that in time we withdraw from Communion and give up our private prayer. . . . [A soul] loses confidence and sits with her hands in her lap because she thinks she can do nothing well. . . ." (*Way of Perfection* XXXIX.1)

4. "'Peace, peace,' said the Lord. . . Uunless we have peace, and strive for peace in our own home, we shall not find it in the homes of others. Let this war now cease. By the blood which Christ shed for us, I beg this of those who have not begun to enter within themselves; and those who have begun to do so must not allow such warfare to turn them back. . . . Let them place their trust, not in their themselves, but in the mercy of God, and they will see how His Majesty can lead them on from one groups of Mansions to another and set them on safe ground. . . ." (*Interior Castle* II.i.10)

Chapter 13
The Little Maid Learns Some Lessons

Narration

After the oral reading of this chapter is complete, take turns narrating the events of this chapter.

Parallel Figures Chart

foot slipped in crossing the road
car came and drove over you

Checking the Catechism

Vicar of Christ
forgive
contrition (perfect and imperfect)

Discussion Topics

1. If you commit a venial sin, what is the best thing to do? List some things you can do to prevent a venial sin—or a small bad habit—from becoming a mortal sin.
2. Why is it important to make a good act of contrition after committing any sin?

Searching Scripture

Sirach 30:8   John 12:24-26
Luke 16:10   Galatians 5:16-26

Growing in Holiness

Try to please Jesus in all you do. When you find yourself being selfish, disobedient, or sulky, make a good act of contrition and begin anew immediately. Jesus is ready to forgive us as soon as we ask. He never tires of forgiving us, as His love is perfect and true.

❝❞ Carmelite Connections

1. "... We shall learn to subdue our wills in everything; for if ... you are very careful *about your prayer*, you will *soon* find yourselves gradually reaching the summit of the mountain without knowing how. But how harsh it sounds to say that we must take pleasure in nothing, unless we also say what consolations and delights this renunciation brings in its train, and what a great gain it is, even in this life! (*Way of Perfection* XII.3)

2. "But it is one thing to commit a sin knowingly and after long deliberation, and quite another to do it so suddenly that the knowledge of its being a venial sin and its commission are one and the same thing, and we hardly realize what we have done. ... *Remember the importance of habit and of starting to realize what a serious thing it is to offend Him* ... for our life, and much more than our life, depends upon this virtue [fear of the Lord] being firmly planted in our souls. Until you are conscious within your soul of possessing it, you need always to exercise very great care and to avoid all occasions of sin and any kind of company which will not help you to get nearer to God. Be most careful, in all that you do, to bend your will to it; see that all you say tends to edification; flee from all places where there is conversation which is not thoroughly impressed upon the soul; though, if one has true love, it is quickly acquired." (*Way of Perfection* XLI.5-6)

3. "... an obedience so *extremely* strict that we never go an inch beyond the superior's orders, knowing that these orders come from God. ... It is to this duty of obedience that you must attach the greatest importance." (*Way of Perfection* XVIII.7)

4. ". . . When the way of perfection was opened out before me, I realised that in order to become a Saint one must suffer much, always seek the most perfect path, and forget oneself. I also understood that there are many degrees of holiness, that each soul is free to respond to the calls of Our Lord, to do much or little for His Love—in a word, to choose amongst the sacrifices He asks." (*Story of a Soul*, Chapter I)

Chapter 14
What the King Loved in the Little Maid

Narration

After the oral reading of this chapter is complete, take turns narrating the events of this chapter.

Parallel Figures Chart

brave little soldier

✓ Checking the Catechism

Eighth Commandment
truth
despair
Perfections of God—especially all-present and all-knowing

Discussion Topics

1. What were some of the traits the King loved in Dilecta? What do you think are some of the things He loves about you?
2. Why was Jesus pleased with Dilecta even though she gave in to her anger? Why is it important to keep trying even when we sin?

Searching Scripture

Psalms 37:1-11
Mark 8:34-38
Colossians 3:23
Luke 12:6-9
1 Corinthians 9:24-26

✠ Growing in Holiness

As you make your examination of conscience each night before bedtime, try to recall all the times you fought off sin and avoided the occasions or conditions that cause you to sin. Thank Jesus as well as your guardian angel for helping you to persevere in the battle against sin. Trust in God and His mercy. Never give up the fight against sin!

" " Carmelite Connections

1. "[God] will also manifest very clearly that he alone is truth and cannot lie. . . . If we are in any way to grow like our God. . .we shall do well always to study earnestly to walk in this truth. I do not mean simply that we must not tell falsehoods. . . . I mean that we should walk in truth, in the presence of God and man, in every way possible to us. In particular we must not desire to be reputed better than we are and in all we do we must attribute to God what is His and to ourselves what is ours, and try to seek after truth in everything. If we do that, we shall make small account of this world, for it is all lying and falsehood and for that reason cannot endure." (*Interior Castle* VI.x.5-6)

2. ". . . This King, Who, unskilled though I am in speaking with Him, does not refuse to hear me or forbid me to approach Him, or command His guards to throw me out. For the angels in His presence know well that their King is such that He prefers the unskilled language of a humble peasant boy, knowing that he would say more if he had more to say, to the speech of the wisest and most learned men, however elegant may be their arguments, if these are not accompanied by humility. But we must not be unmannerly because He is good. . . . When you approach God, then, try to think and realize Whom you are about to address and continue to do so while you are addressing Him. If we had a thousand lives, we should

never fully understand how this Lord merits that we behave toward Him, before Whom even the angels tremble. He orders all things and He can do all things; with Him to will is to perform. . . . Do not, I beg you, address God while you are thinking of other things. . . ." (*Way of Perfection* XXII.4, 7-8)

3. "Another reason [for beginning with determination] . . . is that a resolute person fights more courageously. He knows that, come what may, he must not retreat. He is like a soldier in battle who is aware that if he is vanquished, his life will not be spared and that if he escapes death in battle he must die afterwards. *It has been proved, I think, that* such a man will fight more resolutely and will try, as they say, to sell his life dearly, fearing the enemy's blows the less because he understands the importance of victory and knows that his very life depends upon his gaining it." (*Way of Perfection* XXIII.5)

4. "It will profit me little if I am alone and deeply recollected, and make acts of love to Our Lord and plan and promise to work wonders in His service, and then, as soon as I leave my retreat and some occasion presents itself, I do just the opposite. . . . For, when He sees a very timorous soul, He sends it . . . some very sore trial . . . and later, when the soul becomes aware of this, it loses its fear and offers itself to Him the more readily." (*Interior Castle* VII.iv.7)

Chapter 15
How the King Found the Little Maid Sad One Day

Narration
After the oral reading of this chapter is complete, take turns narrating the events of this chapter.

Parallel Figures Chart
princesses

✓ Checking the Catechism
Stations of the Cross
envy

Discussion Topics
1. The King compares His love to the sunshine. What other comparisons can you make for His love?
2. Read Saint Paul's treatise on love in 1 Corinthians 13:4-7. Choose one characteristic of love from this passage. Write or discuss how you might live out that love within your daily family life.

Searching Scripture
Luke 6:27-35
John 13:34-35
Ephesians 5:10
Luke 10:3
Romans 12:1-2

✚ Growing in Holiness

If possible, go to a church or chapel and pray the Stations of the Cross. Or use a Stations of the Cross meditation book to perform this devotion at home. Share, each day, the day's events and your struggles in serving Jesus with Him. Remember that He wants to hear not only about your successes in conquering sin but also your failures—not only of your love for Him but also of all the tiny details of your day. Make little presents to Him throughout the day by offering Him your sacrifices, your trials, and your thanksgivings.

❝❞ Carmelite Connections

1. "As the sun shines both on the cedar and on the floweret, so the Divine Sun illumines every soul, great and small. . . ." (*Story of a Soul*, Chapter I)

2. ". . . the Father of lights . . . Who, like the sun's ray, sheds His blessings abundantly without respect of persons, wheresoever there is cause, showing Himself likewise joyfully to men as they walk in the roads and paths . . . all over the round earth." (*Living Flame* I.15)

3. ". . . You must not despise this first favour . . . even though you have not responded immediately to the Lord's call; for His Majesty is quite prepared to wait many days and even years, especially when He sees we are persevering and have good desires. This is the most necessary thing . . . [in the second mansions]; if we have this, we can not fail to gain greatly. Nevertheless, the assault which the devils now make upon the soul, in all kinds of ways, is terrible; and the soul suffers more than in the preceding Mansions. . . ." (*Interior Castle* II.i.4)

Dilecta is entering the illuminative stage and the third Teresian mansion. She is making Jesus the center of her life. She is beginning to imitate Him and is growing in virtue. Characteristic of the third mansions, she is careful not to offend God, avoiding even venial sins. Her love for penance is growing, and she is cautious of her speech. Many spend much time in the first three mansions: "It seems that, in order to reach these Mansions [the fourth and beyond], one must have lived for a long time in the others." (*Interior Castle* V.i.1)

(Note that the illuminative way roughly corresponds to the fourth through sixth Teresian mansions.)

Chapter 16
The Golden City

Narration
After the oral reading of this chapter is complete, take turns narrating the events of this chapter.

Parallel Figures Chart
own country   a work to do
palace   lens

✔ Checking the Catechism
Blessed Virgin

Discussion Topics
1. St. Augustine stated, "You have made us for Yourself, and our heart is restless until it rests in You." Explain this statement in light of the content of this chapter.
2. What does Jesus tell Dilecta about the gift of faith? What does this gift enable her—and us—to do? How can the light of faith be kept bright?

Searching Scripture
Psalm 118:24   Hebrews 13:14
1 Corinthians 13:12   Matthew 24:36-44
Matthew 6:19-21   Revelation 12:1
2 Corinthians 3:18   Matthew 25:21
Matthew 7:21   Revelation 21:1-27
Ephesians 2:19-22   Luke 12:15
Matthew 19:23-24

✝ Growing in Holiness

In this chapter, Jesus complains to Dilecta that many people neglect the task of perfecting themselves. Instead many people spend their time and energy gathering possessions and do nothing but enjoy themselves. In Scripture too, Jesus cautions us against storing up treasures that are not heavenly treasures. Do a thorough inventory of your priorities—not what you say your priorities are but what your actions and lifestyle reveal them to be. If you are not busy preparing yourself for your heavenly home but rather are making yourself very comfortable here on earth, maybe you need to make some changes. What can you do differently to ensure that your salvation, and the salvation of others, is a higher priority?

" Carmelite Connections

1. "... Imagine that we have within us a palace of priceless worth, built entirely of gold and precious stones—a palace . . . fit for so great a Lord. Imagine that it is partly your doing that this palace should be what it is—and this is really true, for there is no building so beautiful as a soul that is pure and full of virtues, and, the greater the virtues are, the more brilliantly do the stones shine. Imagine that within the palace dwells this great King . . . Who is seated upon a throne of supreme price—namely, your heart." (*Way of Perfection* XXVIII.10)
2. "... The Lord knows everyone as he really is and gives each his work to do—according to what He sees to be most fitting for his soul, and for His own Self, and for the good of his neighbour. . . . It is well that the Lord should see that we are not leaving anything undone." (*Way of Perfection* XVIII.3)
3. "... Death has come to many people I knew then, young, rich, and happy. I recall to mind the delightful places where they lived, and ask myself where they are

now, and what profit they derive today from the beautiful houses and grounds where I saw them enjoying all the good things of this life, and I reflect that 'All is vanity besides loving God and serving Him alone.'" (*Story of a Soul*, Chapter IV)

4. "Oh, what a mockery is everything in the world if it does not lead us and help us towards this end—and would be even though all the worldly delights and riches and joys that we can imagine were to last forever! For everything is cloying and degrading by comparison with these treasures, which we shall enjoy eternally. And even these are nothing by comparison with having for our own the Lord of all treasures and of Heaven and earth." (*Interior Castle* VI.iv.10)

5. "You are really the daughters of Our Lady. . . . Imitate Our Lady and consider how great she must be. . . ." (*Interior Castle* III.i.3)

6. "He [the King] reveals Himself to those whom He knows will profit by His presence; though unseen by bodily eyes, He has many ways of revealing Himself to the soul through deep inward emotions and by various other means." (*Way of Perfection* XXXIV.11)

7. ". . . Reason tells the soul how mistaken it is in thinking that all these earthly things are of the slightest value by comparison with what it is seeking; faith instructs it in what it must do to find satisfaction; memory shows it how all these things come to an end, and reminds it that those who have derived too much enjoyment from the things which it has seen have died. Sometimes they have died suddenly and been quickly forgotten by all." (*Interior Castle* II.i.5)

8. ". . . teaching me where our true home is and . . . showing me that on earth we are but pilgrims; it is a great thing to see what is awaiting us there and to know where we are going to live. For if a person has to go and settle in another country, it is a great help to him in bearing

the trials of the journey if he has found out that it is a country where he will be able to live in complete comfort. It also makes it easy for us to die if we think upon heavenly things and try to have our conversation in Heaven. This is a great advantage for us: merely to look up towards the heavens makes the soul recollected, for, as the Lord has been pleased to reveal some part of what is there, the thought dwells upon it." (*Life of the Holy Mother Teresa of Jesus* XXXVIII.6)

9. "... When we are wearied with travelling ... the Lord grants ... our soul quiet, and while they are in that state He gives us a clear understanding of the nature of the gifts He bestows upon those whom He brings to His Kingdom ... which will give them a great hope of eventually attaining to a perpetual enjoyment of what on earth He only allows them to taste." (*Way of Perfection* XXX.7)

Chapter 17
The Land of Weary Waiting

Narration
After the oral reading of this chapter is complete, take turns narrating the events of this chapter.

Parallel Figures Chart
terrible things she saw
Land of Weary Waiting

✓ Checking the Catechism
Purgatory
hell
judgment (particular and general)

Discussion Topics
1. What were the three directions in which Dilecta could turn her lens? How might our thoughts and actions be different if we too could see these things?
2. Describe the pains of Purgatory. How can we avoid them? What can we do to aid the many suffering souls in Purgatory?
3. Why must we prize the gift of faith?

Searching Scripture
2 Maccabees 12:42-46   Luke 17:5-6
1 Corinthians 3:13-15   Revelation 20:12-15

Growing in Holiness
Offer up your prayers, actions, and sacrifices each day for the holy souls in Purgatory. Pray for them when you pass a

cemetery. Add a simple prayer for them after your mealtime prayer or within your morning or evening prayers. Ask your guardian angel (*Angel* means "messenger.") to deliver these prayers and sacrifices to the suffering souls.

" Carmelite Connections

1. "Then [in heaven] we shall be amazed to see how different His judgment is from the ideas which we have formed on earth." (*Interior Castle* VI.viii.10)
2. "Lord, how Thou doest afflict Thy lovers. . . . It is well that great things should cost a great deal, especially if the soul can be purified by suffering and enabled to enter the seventh Mansion, just as those who are to enter Heaven are cleansed in purgatory." (*Interior Castle* VI.xi.6)
3. "How sweet will be the death of those who have done penance for all their sins and have not to go to purgatory! It may be that they will begin to enjoy glory even in this world, and will know no fear, but only peace." (*Way of Perfection* XL.9)
4. ". . . How much more sensitive the soul is than the body . . . This suffering resembles that of souls in purgatory; despite their being no longer in the body they suffer much more than do those who are still in the body and on earth." (*Interior Castle* VI.xi.3)
5. ". . . Let us consider the condition of those who are in hell. . . . The torment suffered by the soul is much more acute than that suffered by the body. . . . These unhappy souls know that they will have to suffer in this way forever and ever. . . ." (*Interior Castle* VI.xi.7)
6. "What does it matter if I am in Purgatory until the Day of Judgment provided a single soul should be saved through my prayer? And how much less does it matter if many souls profit by it and the Lord is honoured!" (*Way of Perfection* III.6)

Chapter 18
Brave Love

Narration
After the oral reading of this chapter is complete, take turns narrating the events of this chapter.

Parallel Figures Chart
save up her pennies

✓ Checking the Catechism
corporal and spiritual works of mercy
Dark night of the soul

Discussion Topics
1. How important is it to feel the presence (and presents) of Jesus?
2. Why must we persevere even when we do not feel like we are making progress in the spiritual life or doing anything at all to please Jesus?
3. What role do both silence and feelings play in our prayer life?

Searching Scripture
Matthew 10:40-42
Matthew 25:34-46
Read at least three of the following psalms: Psalm 27, Psalm 42:1-6, Psalm 62, Psalm 63, Psalm 116, Psalm 131, Psalm 139, or Psalm 150.

✝ Growing in Holiness

Try to receive Jesus in the Blessed Sacrament every day. Visit Him in the tabernacle as often as possible. Remember to watch for His face, not His hands when He comes to you; bring gifts to Him rather than watching for His gifts to you. Try to advance in the spiritual life so that the most important thing for you is not your own feelings of happiness and peace but the satisfaction of knowing that you are pleasing Him even though you do not feel His peace nor His presence.

❝❞ Carmelite Connections

1. "For often it is God's will that His elect should be conscious of their misery and so He withdraws His help from them a little—and no more than that is needed to make us recognize our limitations very quickly. They then realize that this is a way of testing them, for they gain a clear perception of their shortcomings, and sometimes they derive more pain from finding that, in spite of themselves, they are still grieving about earthly things, and not very important things either, than from the matter which is troubling them. This, I think, is a great mercy on the part of God, and even though they are at fault they gain a great deal in humility." (*Interior Castle* III.ii.2)

2. "Having won such great favours, the soul . . . has the keenest longings for death, and so it frequently and tearfully begs God to take it out of this exile. Everything in this life that it sees wearies it; when it finds itself alone it experiences great relief, but immediately this distress returns till it hardly knows itself when it is without it." (*Interior Castle* VI.vi.1)

3. "[The King] never takes His eyes off you. . . . He has borne with thousands of foul and abominable sins which you have committed against him, yet even they

have not been enough to make Him cease looking upon you. Is it such a great matter, then, for you to avert the eyes of your soul from outward things and sometimes to look at Him? See, He is only waiting for us to look at Him. He longs so much for us to look at Him once more that it will not be for lack of effort on His part if we fail to do so." (*Way of Perfection* XXVI.3)

4. Referring to those souls in the fourth mansions, St. Teresa states, "A person who used to be afraid of doing penance . . . now believes that in God he can to everything, and has more desire to do such things than he had previously. The fear of trials that he was wont to have is now largely assuaged, because he has a more lively faith, and realizes that, if he endures these trials for God's sake, His Majesty will give him grace to bear them patiently, and sometimes even to desire them, because he also cherishes a great desire to do something for God. The better he gets to know the greatness of God, the better he comes to realize the misery of his own condition; having now tasted the consolations of God, he sees that earthly things are mere refuse; so, little by little, he withdraws from them and in this way becomes more his own master. In short, he finds himself strengthened in all the virtues and will infallibly continue to increase in them unless he turns back and commits offences against God." (*Interior Castle* IV.iii.9)

Dilecta is now in the classical unitive stage of perfection as characterized by the habitual, intimate union with God through Jesus; a delight in prayer; living continually in the presence of God; great mastery over self; constant loving and lingering thoughts of God; all virtues infused with love; and a simplification of her life in that prayer is no longer at set times but permeates her whole life.

Chapter 19
The King in His Beauty

Narration
After the oral reading of this chapter is complete, take turns narrating the events of this chapter.

Parallel Figures Chart
training to come to an end
come in your disguise to the little hut

✓ Checking the Catechism
death
Second Coming of Christ

Discussion Topics
1. Describe the ways in which Dilecta trained Self. In what ways was Self becoming better behaved? In what ways does your Self need more training? List at least three ways that you can work with your Self in order to have him/her better trained.
2. List too several ways in which you can try to know and love Jesus better: "Do not grow slack in zeal, be fervent in spirit, serve the Lord" (Romans 12:11).

Searching Scripture
Psalm 24
2 Timothy 4:6-8
Psalm 122:1
James 1:12
Matthew 16:27
1 Peter 5:4
Mark 13:32-37

✠ Growing in Holiness

Based upon the prayer of the little maid as she viewed Jesus face-to-face, prepare a short prayer of thanksgiving for Jesus' presence in the Holy Eucharist. Recite this prayer either before receiving Communion or immediately after its reception.

❝❞ Carmelite Connections

1. "Once our debts have been paid we shall be able to walk in safety. We shall not be going into a foreign land, but into our own country, for it belongs to Him Whom we have loved so truly and Who Himself loves us." (*Way of Perfection* XL.8)

2. ". . . I was weary of earthly pilgrimages and only longed for the beauties of Heaven." (*Story of a Soul*, Chapter VI)

3. "But how shall I show my love, since love proves itself by deeds? Well! The little child will strew flowers. . . . She will embrace the Divine Throne with their fragrance, she will sing Love's Canticle in silvery tones. Yes, my Beloved, it is thus my short life shall be spent in Thy sight. The only way I have of proving my love is to strew flowers before Thee—that is to say, I will let no tiny sacrifice pass, no look, no word. I wish to profit by the smallest actions, and to do them for Love. I wish to suffer for Love's sake, and for Love's sake even to rejoice: thus shall I strew flowers. Not one shall I find without scattering its petals before Thee. . . . and I will sing. . . . I will sing always, even if my roses must be gathered from amidst thorns; and the longer and sharper the thorns, the sweeter shall be my song. But of what avail to thee, my Jesus, are my flowers and my songs? I know it well: this fragrant shower, these delicate petals of little price, these songs of love from a poor little heart like mine, will

nevertheless be pleasing unto Thee. Trifles they are, but Thou wilt smile on them. The Church Triumphant, stooping towards her child, will gather up these scattered rose leaves, and, placing them in Thy Divine Hands, there to acquire an infinite value, will shower them on the Church Suffering to extinguish its flames, and on the Church Militant to obtain its victory." (*Story of a Soul*, Chapter XI)

4. ". . . It was folly to come and seek the poor hearts of mortal men to make them thrones for Him, the King of Glory, Who sitteth above the Cherubim! Was He not supremely happy in the company of His Father and the Holy Spirit of Love? Why, then, come down on earth to seek sinners and make of them His closest friends? Nay, our folly could never exceed His. . . ." (*Story of a Soul*, Letter to Celine, XX)

5. "I seem already to touch the Heavenly Shore and to receive Our Lord's embrace. I fancy I can see Our Blessed Lady coming to meet me . . . and I picture myself enjoying true family joys for all eternity." (*Story of a Soul*, Chapter IV)

6. ". . . I never on any occasion saw more than the Lord was pleased to show me. What I saw was so great that the smallest part of it was sufficient to leave my soul amazed and to do it so much good that it esteemed and considered all the things of this life as of little worth. I wish I could give a description of at least the smallest part of what I learned, but, when I try to discover a way of doing so, I find it impossible; for, while the light we see here and that other light are both light, there is no comparison between the two and the brightness of the sun seems quite dull if compared with the other. In short, however skillful the imagination may be, it will not succeed in picturing or describing what that light is like, nor a single one of those things which I learned from the Lord with a joy so sovereign as to be indescrib-

able. For all the senses rejoice in a high degree, and with a sweetness impossible to describe, for which reason it is better to say no more about it." (*Life of the Holy Mother Teresa of Jesus* XXXVIII.2)

7. "And thus this soul . . . at the gates of the palace . . . is recompensed . . . in a single day for all its trials and services, for not only is it made to enter the palace and stand before the King, clothed in regal vesture, but likewise it is crowned, and given a scepter, and a royal seat, and possession of the royal ring, so that it may do all that it desires, and need do naught that it desires not to do in the kingdom of its Spouse; for those that are in this state receive all that they desire." (*Living Flame,* Second Redaction, II.31)

The King of the
Golden City

Study Guide
Answer Key

Answer Key for
The King of the Golden City Study Guide

(Note that there may be many different "correct answers" for any of these figures. There are other possible allegorical figures. The answers below represent possible figures and meanings; do not feel limited to them.)

Chapter 1—The Meeting in the Wood
the King—Jesus
the country of the travelers (Land of Exile)—earth
the Golden City—our heavenly home
the rebel lord Malignus—Satan, the devil
the Happy Ones—the saints in heaven
the maid—each of us
the maid's hut—the maid's body, her heart (our bodies, our hearts)
the wildflowers—virtues practiced and sacrifices made
the King's simple robe of white—Jesus' appearance in the Host
the path to the hut—our preparation for Holy Communion
quarter of an hour spent within the hut together—the time of His physical presence with each of us after receiving Him in Holy Communion, our time of thanksgiving after Communion
the unclean hut—our soul when it is not adequately prepared to receive Him in Communion
no fit spot to lay them (the King's gifts) *down*—a soul not adequately prepared to receive Him or a soul in the state of sin
the wounds of the King—His sufferings and wounds obtained on the cross for us

Chapter 2—The Little Maid Finds She Must Help in Her Training
lieutenants—the pope and other bishops
prince of the Court (Prince Guardian)—guardian angel

teachers—priests, CCD teachers, parents, Holy Scripture, the Church, our guardian angel

Chapter 3—The King's Laws
signs—commandments, Church laws, precepts of Scripture and the sacraments
the straight road—the way of the Cross, following Jesus, the way of grace

Chapter 4—The King's Household
a large House—the Catholic Church and the treasury of the Church
the School—the teachings and doctrines of the Church, the catechism, Holy Scripture
the Gymnasium—the family
the Armory—the Sacrament of Confirmation
the Hospital or Infirmary—the Sacraments of Reconciliation and Anointing of the Sick
the Banquet Hall—the Sacrament of the Eucharist
the Royal Audience Chamber—the church where Mass is held and the tabernacle resides

Chapter 5—A Troublesome Partner
Self—our self-love, our free will, our tendency toward sin, our conscience, temptations of the flesh
lamp of "Peace"—God's gift of grace, His life in us, the theological virtues of faith, hope and love

Chapter 6—The King's Table
daily banquet—the great gift of daily reception of our Lord in Holy Communion
the white robe—our soul in the state of grace
ante-chamber—confessional
small stains on the white robe—venial sins
jewels with which the King adorned the white robe—grace

Chapter 7—Dilecta Asks for a Change
Bridget—a person who has stayed true to Jesus despite adversity and temptation; a virtuous person willing to carry the cross of suffering

Chapter 8—The King's Armory
Soldiers of the Royal Army—confirmed members of the Catholic Church

enrolled in my Army—confirmed in the Church, a soldier of Christ

Jolly Ones or Triflers—those not concerned about life everlasting; non-Christians or non-practicing Christians; the temptations of the world

Chapter 9—The King's Infirmary
wounded soldiers—those with unconfessed sins on their souls

sullied white robe—the soul of those with unpardoned sins on their souls

Chapter 10—The Little Maid in an Idle Mood
master of his own house—master of his own soul, one with a well-formed conscience and strong will

soft knock at the door—subtle tempting of Satan; temptation; near occasion of sin

Chapter 11—The Broad Road
the fair—the world where both Christians and non-Christians live together where it is necessary to discern which activities and amusements are appropriate for a follower of Christ; the place where pleasure reigns and tempts

the play—pleasures that are not Christian; sinful activities

Daisy—peer pressure

the broad road—time-wasting pleasures that do not bring us closer to Jesus and are not pleasing to Him; temptations of the world

Chapter 12—The Fair
bad sweets sprinkled with sugar—thoughts or actions that appear on the outside, without much thought or observation, to be harmless that are, in fact, not so
poisonous powders—evil thoughts; sacrilegious ideas; impure thoughts
Dark Valley—God's seat of Justice where the punishments of the dead are given; first step toward Purgatory or hell

Chapter 13—The Little Maid Learns Some Lessons
foot slipped in crossing the road—venial sin
car came and drove over you—mortal sin

Chapter 14—What the King Loved in the Little Maid
brave little soldier—a soldier of Christ; someone who fights to become more like Jesus every day and bears his cross as Christ did

Chapter 15—How the King Found the Little Maid Sad One Day
princesses—female Christians striving to imitate Jesus so as to be crowned by Him in death (Male Christians would be *princes*.)

Chapter 16—The Golden City
own country—our home in heaven
palace—that part of heaven, the new Jerusalem, where God sits upon the throne
a work to do—our growth in grace; the process of our sanctification; the use of our gifts to further the kingdom of God
lens—our vision through the eyes of faith

Chapter 17—The Land of Weary Waiting
terrible things she saw—hell
Land *of Weary Waiting*—Purgatory

Chapter 18—Brave Love

save up her pennies—offer her merits and indulgences for the holy souls in Purgatory even at the cost of having none left for herself

Chapter 19—The King in His Beauty

training to come to an end—our Christian training and love for Jesus, which causes us to desire to be like Jesus and to please Him in all things; ends only with our death
come in your disguise to the little hut—Jesus as plain Bread coming into our hearts in Holy Communion

Additional Parallel Figures

Chapter Number	Event, Person or Object	Parallel Figure

Parables of Jesus,
Readings for Each Chapter of
The King of the Golden City

Chapter 1
Remember that a parable is similar to an allegory. Jesus taught moral lessons by using allegories and parables. Today read Jesus' explanation of the purpose of His parables: Matthew 13:10-15 and Matthew 13:34-35. Read, too, the Old Testament prophecy regarding the need to pass these parables on to the next generation: Psalm 78:1-8. Meditate upon how you can use this information when studying an allegory such as *The King of the Golden City* as well as in our study of the parables of Jesus and their application to our daily lives.

Chapter 2
Read the parable with the theme of the reward of working for God: the laborers in the vineyard, Matthew 20:1-16.

Chapter 3
Read the parables with the theme of the Kingdom of God on earth: the mustard seed, Matthew 13:31-32 **or** Mark 4:30-32 **or** Luke 13:18-19; the leaven, Luke 13:20-21; and the treasure hidden in a field, Matthew 13:44.

Chapter 4
Continue reading the parables regarding the Kingdom of God on earth: the pearl of great value, Matthew 13:45-46; the net cast into the sea, Matthew 13:47-50; and the seed cast onto the earth, Mark 4:26-29.

Chapter 5
Read the parable about doing the will of God: two sons, Matthew 21:28-31.

Chapter 6
Read the parables that have the theme of the abuse of God's grace: the wedding feast, Matthew 22:1-14; and the great supper, Luke 14:15-24.

Chapter 7
Read the parable with the theme of the power of prayer: the judge and the widow, Luke 18:1-8.

Chapter 8
Read the parables with the theme of working for God and for heaven: the parable of the talents, Matthew 25:14-30; and the parable of the pounds, Luke 19:11-27.

Chapter 9
Read the parable on the forgiveness of sins: the prodigal son, Luke 15:11-32.

Chapter 10
Read the parables that have the theme of God's patience in His dealings with sinners: the weeds among the wheat, Matthew 13:24-30, 36-43; and the barren fig tree, Luke 13:6-9.

Chapter 11
Read the parable that has the theme of the rejection of Christ: the parable of the tenants, Matthew 21:33-44. **or** Mark 12:1-12 **or** Luke 20:9-19.

Chapter 12
Read the parable of Christ's love for us: the good shepherd, John 10:1-18.

Chapter 13
Read the parable with the theme of gratitude for the forgiveness of sins: the forgiven debtors, Luke 7:40-43.

Chapter 14
Read the parable with the theme of forgiving injuries: the unforgiving servant, Matthew 18:21-35.

Chapter 15
Read the parable that reflects on humility and pride: the Pharisee and the tax collector, Luke 18:9-14.

Chapter 16
Read the parables that deal with use of riches: the dishonest steward, Luke 16:1-8; and the rich man and Lazarus, Luke 16:19-31.

Chapter 17
Read the parable that tells us about love of our neighbor: the good Samaritan, Luke 10:29-37.

Chapter 18
Read the parables that tell us of Christ's love for sinners: the lost sheep, Matthew 18:12-14 **or** Luke 15:1-7; and the lost coin, Luke 15:8-10.

Chapter 19
Read the parables that have the theme of watchfulness and preparation for the judgment: vigilant and faithful servants, Matthew 24:45-51 **or** Luke 12:35-40, 41-46; the ten virgins, Matthew 25:1-13; and the rich fool, Luke 12:16-21.

Scripture and Deep Prayer

The following biblical passages underscore the frequency with which both the Old and New Testaments discuss the phenomenon of deep prayer:

Old Testament References to Prayer

1. Job 43:5
2. Psalm 1:1-2
3. Psalm 36:8-10
4. Psalm 25:15
5. Psalm 27:4
6. Psalm 34:5
7. Psalm 34:9
8. Psalm 42:2-3
9. Psalm 42:8
10. Psalm 62:2
11. Psalm 63:2-3
12. Psalm 77:3
13. Psalm 84:2-3
14. Psalm 119:10
15. Psalm 139:7-10
16. Isaiah 30:15
17. Ezekiel 16:14

New Testament References to Prayer

1. Matthew 6:6-8
2. Mark 1:35
3. Luke 2:19
4. Luke 5:16
5. Luke 6:12
6. Luke 10:21
7. John 15:4-5
8. Romans 5:5
9. Romans 8:26
10. 1 Corinthians 2:9
11. 1 Corinthians 10:31
12. 2 Corinthians 3:18
13. 2 Corinthians 5:17
14. 2 Corinthians 12:2-3
15. Galatians 2:20
16. Ephesians 3:14-19
17. Colossians 1:9
18. Colossians 2:2-3
19. James 1:4
20. 1 Peter 1:8
21. 1 John 2:6
22. 1 John 3:24
23. 1 John 4:12
24. 1 John 4:16

Recommended Reading

In closing the Jubilee Year of 2000, Pope John Paul II—in his apostolic letter *Novo Millennio Ineunte*—urged us to learn *the art of prayer* (32) and asks, "How can we forget here, among the many shining examples, the teachings of Saint John of the Cross and Saint Teresa of Avila?" (33) The resources below will provide much instruction on this "art of prayer" from the Carmelite Doctors of the Church.

Collected Works of St. John of the Cross, translated by Kieran Kavanaugh and Otilio Rodriguez, ICS Publications, 1991.

Collected Works of St. Teresa of Avila – Volumes 1, 2, and 3, translated by Kieran Kavanaugh and Otilio Rodriguez, ICS Publications, 1976, 1980, and 1985. [Volume 2 of this edition of *The Interior Castle* contains a table of castle imagery with allegorical applications similar to the parallel figures chart in *The King of the Golden City Study Guide.*]

Conversation with Christ: An Introduction to Mental Prayer by Fr. Peter-Thomas Rohrbach, 1956. [This book has been republished by Tan Books and Publishers, Inc.]

Deep Conversion, Deep Prayer by Thomas Dubay, Ignatius Press, 2006.

Fire Within: St. Teresa of Avila, St. John of the Cross, and the Gospel—on Prayer by Fr. Thomas Dubay, Ignatius Press, 1989.

Fulfillment of All Desire: A Guidebook for the Journey to God Based on the Wisdom of the Saints by Ralph Martin, Emmaus Road, 2006.

God Speaks in the Night: The Life, Times, and Teaching of St. John of the Cross, ICS Publications, 1991, 2000. [A photo journal]

Lectio Divina and the Practice of Teresian Prayer by Sam Anthony Morello, ICS Publications, 1995.

Prayer Primer: Igniting the Fire Within by Thomas Dubay, Ignatius Press, 2002.

Saint Teresa of Avila: A Spiritual Adventure by Tomas
   Alvarez, ICS Publications, 1982. [A photo journal]
Story of a Soul Study Edition, translated by John Clarke, text
   prepared by Marc Foley, ICS Publications, 2005.
Therese and Lisieux, translated by Salvatore and Louise
   Pambrun, Eerdmans, 1996. [A photo journal]
When the Lion Roars: A Primer for the Unsuspecting Mystic
   by Stephen J. Rossetti, Ave Maria Press, 2003.
Way of Perfection Study Edition, text prepared by Kieran
   Kavanaugh, ICS Publications, 2000.

Quotations from St. Teresa of Avila within *The King of
the Golden City Study Guide* are excerpted from *The Complete Works of St. Teresa of Jesus*, translated by Allison Peers,
Sheed & Ward, 1946. This public domain work is available
online.

Quotations from St. Therese of the Child Jesus are excerpted
from *The Story of a Soul* as translated by Thomas Taylor.
This work is also available online.

Quotations from St. John of the Cross are excerpted from
The Complete Works of St. John of the Cross, translated by
Allison Peers, Sheed & Ward, 1949.

For more in-depth study of the Carmelite Doctors of the Church,
read the works as translated by Kavanaugh and Rodriguez
for St. Teresa and St. John and those by John Clarke for St.
Therese of the Child Jesus. The website for the publisher of
these books—the Institute for Carmelite Studies Publications—is www.icspublications.org.

For further information about Carmelite spirituality, the
secular (third) order, and secular order community locations,
visit this website: www.secularcarmelite.com. ("Helpful
Links" gives information on each of the three US OCDS
provinces and their communities.)

Other RACE for Heaven Products

Catholic Study Guides for Mary Fabyan Windeatt's Saint Biography Series teach the Catholic faith to all members of your family. Written with your family's various learning levels in mind, these flexible study guides succeed as stand-alone unit studies or supplements to your regular curriculum. Thirty to sixty minutes per day will allow your family to experience:

- ☑ The spirituality and holy habits of the saints
- ☑ Lively family discussions on important faith topics
- ☑ Increased critical thinking and reading comprehension skills
- ☑ Quality read-aloud time with Catholic "living books"
- ☑ Enhanced knowledge of Catholic doctrine and the Bible
- ☑ History and geography incorporated into saintly literature
- ☑ Writing projects based on secular and Catholic historical events and characters

Purchase these guides individually or in the following grade-level packages. (Grade level is are determined solely on the length of each book in the series.)

Grades 3-4: *St. Thomas Aquinas, St. Catherine of Siena, Patron Saint of First Communicants,* and *The Miraculous Medal*

Grade 5: *St. Rose, St. Martin de Porres, King David and His Songs,* and *Blessed Marie of New France*

Grade 6: *St. Dominic, St. Benedict, The Children of Fatima and Our Lady's Message to the World;* and *St. John Masias*

Grade 7: *The Little Flower, St. Hyacinth, The Curé of Ars,* and *St. Louis de Montfort*

Grade 8: *Pauline Jaricot, St. Francis Solano, St. Paul the Apostle,* and *St. Margaret Mary*

The Windeatt Dictionary: Pre-Vatican II Terms and Catholic Words from Mary Fabyan Windeatt's Saint Biographies explains over 450 Catholic terms and expressions used in this saint biography series. Indispensable in expanding knowledge and practice of the Catholic faith, this book provides a ready access for the Catholic vocabulary words used in the RACE for Heaven Windeatt study guides. This dictionary also includes a Catholic book report resource that contains suggestions for forty-five Catholic book reports: fourteen writing projects, ten book report activities, and twenty-one topics for saint biographies.

Graced Encounters with Mary Fabyan Windeatt's Saints: 344 Ways to Imitate the Holy Habits of the Saints is a compilation of the "Growing in Holiness" sections of RACE for Heaven's Catholic study guides for the Windeatt saint biography series and presents 344 examples of saintly behavior, one for nearly every chapter in each of these twenty biographies. Enhance your encounter with the saints by practicing the models of devotion, service, penance, prayer, and virtue offered in this guide.

Bedtime Bible Stories for Catholic Children: Loving Jesus through His Word contains twenty discussions of Bible stories that were originally published in serial form in a Catholic children's magazine. The author stated, "The tales are extremely simple and unadorned. They are real conversations of a real child and her mother." Due to popular demand, the series was later (1910) published as a book, *Bible Stories Told to "Toddles."* The engaging conversational style of this book lends itself well as a bedtime read-aloud that allows Jesus to come alive in the Gospels. The study aids include discussion questions to help foster spiritual conversation, Bible excerpts relevant to the presented story, "Growing in Holiness" suggestions for living the Gospel message in our daily lives, and short catechism lessons for both children and adults.

I Talk with God: The Art of Prayer and Meditation for Catholic Children strives to instil in young Catholics a love of prayer and a practical knowledge of the art of meditation. This prayer book contains prayers to pray out loud (vocal prayer) or in the silence of your heart. It shows how to talk with God, and more importantly, how to love God. As children progress through this book—from discovering what prayer is to reading and reciting simple prayers to understanding meditation ("holy thinking") and then to helps for deeper meditation—they will see that prayer and meditation often go together. Discover how to talk with God each day and follow more closely His holy will.

Communion with the Saints: A Family Preparation Program for First Communion and Beyond in the Spirit of St. Therese imitates St. Therese of the Child Jesus and her family who studied and prayed for sixty-nine days in anticipation of Therese's First Holy Communion. Modeling this preparation, the *Communion with the Saints* program will help any family find renewed fervor in the reception of the Eucharist. This resource includes a study of the following four books:

- *The Little Flower, The Story of Saint Therese of the Child Jesus*—to provide the foundation of God's love for us and to encourage a desire for holiness
- *The Children of Fatima and Our Lady's Message to the World*—to show the sinfulness of our world and the need to avoid sin
- *The Patron Saint of First Communicants, The Story of Blessed Imelda Lambertini*—to inspire devotion to the Sacrament of Holy Communion
- *The King of the Golden City* —to illustrate Jesus' Presence as the source of grace necessary to live a holy life

Each of the sixty-nine days of preparation includes read-aloud selections with enrichment activities, meditational readings, catechism lessons, and plenty of practical application to promote a growth in holiness and sanctity. Weekend suggestions include a list of over thirty-five family projects.

My First Communion Journal in Imitation of St. Therese provides a lasting keepsake of a child's First Holy Communion. This journal has been constructed in imitation of the copybook made for Therese Martin by her older sister Pauline. This book contains many of the same prayers and aspirations Therese used, the same idea of flowers inspiring virtue, and the same method of recording prayers recited and sacrifices made. This journal may be completed in conjunction with the *Communion with the Saints* program or used separately.

My First Communion Journal in Imitation of St. Paul, Putting on the Armor of God was also inspired by St. Therese's copybook and uses the same method of encouraging—and recording—daily prayers and mortifications. However, instead of using flowers to illustrate virtues, this resource uses the battle model St. Paul describes in Ephesians 6:10-17. First communicants are encouraged to arm themselves with virtues and spiritual weapons in order to fight as soldiers of Christ.

The King of the Golden City Study Edition is a new edition of a book that was originally published in 1921. This treasure of a book was written in response to a student's appeal for instructions along with "little stories" to help her prepare for Holy Communion. To fulfill this request, Mother Loyola of the Bar Convent in York, England, wrote a simple story that illustrates Jesus' desire to share an intimate relationship with each one of His children. This new edition contains some updated language but, quite deliberately, does not contain any pictures. Readers, as they progress through this story, will form a mental image of their King, one as unique and personal as their own relationship with Him. The study sections assist with the allegory, connect to the Bible as well as to the catechism, and explore the art of prayer in the spirit of the three Carmelite Doctors of the Church. Although written over ninety years ago for a young child, this book remains a timeless masterpiece of Catholic literature suitable for all ages. (Also available as a study guide only)

The Good Shepherd and His Little Lambs Study Edition is a simply told Catholic tale of four children who meet with their beloved aunt for "First Communion talks." More than a story, it is a First Communion primer that takes the tenets of the catechism and, through naturally-flowing conversations, relates them in the language of little ones to authentic Christian living. As Mrs. Bosch explains, "We might learn the catechism all the way through beautifully, and at the end find ourselves still very stiff and clumsy about loving our

Lord." Enriched by appropriate Biblical passages, points of doctrine, and prayers, this story-primer is an enjoyable and effective read-aloud that will prepare the Good Shepherd's little lambs to worthily receive Him in the Holy Eucharist.

A Reconciliation Reader-Retreat: Read-Aloud Lessons, Stories, and Poems for Young Catholics Preparing for Confession provides a basic doctrinal explanation and review of the Sacrament of Reconciliation as well as a Gospel examination of conscience—a seven-day read-aloud formation retreat. Each lesson has been supplemented with pertinent short stories and poems, reflection questions, and a family prayer. A "Gospel Examination of Conscience", formulated according to the dictates of the *Catechism of the Catholic Church*, is included. This reader-retreat will not only enrich and deepen the sacramental experience for each member of your family but it will also provide several tools to help you recommit to leading a virtuous life and to grow together in holiness.

Devotion to St. Joseph: Read-Aloud Stories, Poems, and Prayers for Catholic Children encourages children to love Jesus as St. Joseph did. As Scripture does not record a single word this great saint spoke, we must take our lessons from his actions. In this compilation of stories and poems about our Savior's foster-father from renowned Catholics, children of all ages are encouraged to imitate the virtues of St. Joseph. The discussion questions, reflections on St. Joseph's virtues, and the prayer section promote a lasting devotion to the great St. Joseph. As St. Teresa of Avila declared, "I wish I could persuade everyone to be devoted to this glorious saint!"

The Month of St. Joseph: Prayers and Practices for Each Day of March in Imitation of the Virtues of St. Joseph was originally published in 1874. This book contains daily meditations on the life and virtues of St. Joseph for adults and high-school students. In addition, each day presents a prayer to St. Joseph, several resolutions, a short ejaculatory prayer, a relevant Scripture verse, and a brief consideration for reflection. Perfect for Lenten reading, this journey through the life of St. Joseph reveals his love of God and neighbor, humility, quiet action, and spirit of sacrifice. While the Bible tells so little about St. Joseph's life, here we discover the abundant virtues of this silent saint—and are challenged to imitate them.

Alternative Book Reports for Catholic Students contains forty-five book report ideas to encourage critical thinking for ages seven to fourteen. Many report topics require an examination of our personal faith life and prompt us to take lessons from the saints to strengthen our own faith in God. The suggested activities vary from written exercises to creative art projects and include twenty-one topics specifically designed for saint biographies. Other activities can be used within a group or family.

Reading the Saints: Lists of Catholic Books for Children Plus Book Collecting Tips for the Home and School Library is a valuable tool for Catholic home educators, classroom teachers, and collectors of Catholic juvenile books. This resource will help you discover living books from such popular out-of-print Catholic juvenile series as Catholic Treasury, Vision Books, and American Background Books as well as current series books for young Catholics. Use this book to find:

- Over 800 Catholic books listed by author, series, reading level, century, and geographical location
- More than 275 authors of saint biographies, historical fiction, and poetry written for Catholic juvenile readers
- Publishers of Catholic children's books, present and past
- Helpful advice for collecting and caring for used books
- Hundreds of age-appropriate, accessible living books to enrich your study of the Catholic Church's rich heritage of saints and notable Catholic historical figures
- Information on how to build and maintain your own library of Catholic juvenile books
- Inspiring quotations about book collecting, reading, and the love of books

The Outlaws of Ravenhurst Study Edition contains a classic story of the persecution of Scottish Catholics that was first written in 1923 and was revised and reprinted in 1950. This 2009 edition of Sr. M. Imelda Wallace's story contains the revised story of 1950 plus chapter-by-chapter aids to assist readers in assimilating the book's strong Catholic elements into their own lives. The study section focuses on critical thinking, integration of biblical teachings, and the study of the virtuous life to which Christ calls us as mature Catholics. With its emphasis on virtues (theological and moral plus the gifts and fruits of the Holy Spirit), the spiritual and corporal works of mercy, and the Beatitudes, Outlaws of Ravenhurst Study Edition is a fun and effective catechetical tool for Catholics preparing for the Sacrament of Confirmation. (Also available as a study guide only)

The Family that Overtook Christ Study Edition: The Story of the Family of St. Bernard of Clairvaux is an excellent read for young adults who are preparing to receive the Sacrament of Confirmation. In this exciting chronicle of the life of twelfth-century knights, we have an entire family of nine saints who lay before us their individual means of achieving intimate union with Christ. Learn with the Fontaines family how to supernaturalize the natural, develop a God-consciousness, and attain sanctity by being yourself. Perfect for high-school read-aloud (or adult study), this new study edition has over 250 footnotes for increased comprehension and provides discussion/meditation points to promote the art of spiritual conversation. The appendix lists formulas of Catholic doctrine that are essential for confirmands not only to know but also to incorporate into their own spiritual lives.

A Confirmation Reader-Retreat: Read-Aloud Lessons, Stories and Poems for Young Catholics utilizes chapters from two excellent out-of-print Catholic books for children (*I Belong to God* by Lillian Clark; and *Children's Retreats in Preparation for First Confession, First Holy Communion, and Confirmation* by Rev. P.A. Halpin). This book provides a basic doctrinal review of the Sacrament of Confirmation as well as prayer experiences—a nine-day read-aloud retreat/novena. Supplemented with short stories, poems, and reflection questions, each lesson concludes with "I Talk with God," which encourages readers (of all ages) to deepen their relationship with each of the Three Persons of the Blessed Trinity. Additionally, a traditional novena to the Holy Spirit is included.

By Cross and Anchor Study Edition: The Story of Frederic Baraga on Lake Superior relates the exciting, and often miraculous, missionary adventures of the "Snowshoe Priest"— Venerable Frederic Baraga, the first bishop of Michigan's Upper Peninsula. Declared "Venerable" by Pope Benedict XVI on May 10, 2012, this priest came to the United States from Slovenia in 1830 to undertake his mission as a "simple servant of God." For almost forty years, Fr. Frederic Baraga traveled across over 80,000 square miles of wilder-ness by snowshoe in winter and canoe in summer. In imitation of Christ, Bishop Baraga become poor so that he might bring the riches of the Catholic Faith to the Chippewa and immigrant residents of the beautiful peninsula he served. Although not strictly a biography, this book is a story based on historical facts drawn from Bishop Baraga's own journal and letters—a fascinating, easy-to-read history of Michigan's northern peninsula. While this exciting adventure is intended for youth who are interested in knowing more about this quiet, courageous priest, readers of all ages will be inspired by his life of humility, simplicity, and selfless virtue. This new study edition contains over 130 footnotes, defining less familiar vocabulary words and—gleaned from Venerable Baraga's *Journal* and other primary sources—details regarding the region's people and places. Also in-cluded are discussion questions, applicable Scripture passages, per-tinent quotations of Venerable Baraga from the text, and—most importantly—a section illustrating how to imitate the various virtues of Venerable Frederic Baraga. Additionally, the complete text of Bishop Baraga's 1853 "Pastoral Letter to the Faithful" has been in-cluded with numerous references added in order that we may read this letter in light of Scripture and the *Compendium of the Catechism of the Catholic Church*. Learn more about the life, ministry, and heroic virtues of Venerable Frederic Baraga, the "Snowshoe Priest."

To Order: Email info@RACEforHeaven.com or place an order at RACEforHeaven.com. Discover, MasterCard, VISA, American Express, PayPal, checks, and money orders are accepted.

www.ingramcontent.com/pod-product-compliance
Lightning Source LLC
Chambersburg PA
CBHW060949040426
42445CB00011B/1073